THE
LONGEST
AND
TALLEST

First edition for the United States, Canada,
and the Philippines published 1992
by Barron's Educational Series, Inc.

© Copyright by Aladdin Books Ltd 1992

Design David West Children's Book Design
Illustrator David West
Text Anita Ganeri
Picture research Emma Krikler

Created and designed by
N.W. Books
28 Percy Street
London W1P 9FF

All inquiries should be addressed to:
Barron's Educational Series, Inc.
250 Wireless Boulevard
Hauppauge, NY 11788

International Standard Book No. 0-8120-6293-0

Library of Congress Catalog Card No. 92-12502

Library of Congress Cataloging-in-Publication Data

Ganeri, Anita, 1961-
The longest and tallest / Anita Ganeri.
p.   cm. -- (Questions and answers about--)
Summary: Cartoons and color photographs accompany answers to
questions about some of the longest or tallest record breakers.
ISBN 0-8120-6293-0
1. World records--Miscellanea--Juvenile literature. 2. Children's
questions and answers. [1. World records--Miscellanea.
2. Questions and answers.] I.Title. II. Series: Ganeri, Anita,
1961- Questions and answers about--
AG243.G29 1992
031.02--dc20   92-12502   CIP   AC

Printed in Belgium
234 987654321

QUESTIONS AND ANSWERS ABOUT

THE
LONGEST
AND
TALLEST

Barron's

The Longest and Tallest

The giraffe is a triple record breaker. It is the tallest animal on Earth, growing up to 20 feet (6 meters) high. Giraffes also have the longest legs and the longest necks of any animals in the world. This book will help you learn about some of the other longest and tallest record breakers. They include dinosaurs, bridges, walls and waterfalls, mountains, and musical instruments.

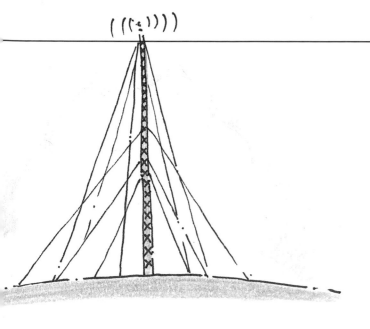

Which is the tallest structure ever built?

The steel radio mast in Plock, Poland is over twice the height of the Eiffel Tower in France and over 500 feet (152 meters) taller than the Sears Tower in Chicago, Illinois. Built in 1974, it is 2,120 feet (646 meters) tall. It is held in place by 15 very strong, steel guy ropes.

Where is the world's longest wall?

The Great Wall of China is about 2,150 miles (3,460 kilometers) long. It was built over 2,000 years ago to keep invaders out of northern China. The wall is between 18 and 30 feet (5 to 9 meters) high, which is taller than three people. According to Chinese legend, the wall is actually a very long dragon that has been turned to stone.

Which is the longest waterfall?

The Angel Falls in Venezuela make up the world's longest waterfall. The water drops 3,211 feet (979 meters) - about as high as a stack of 100 houses. The falls were named after an American pilot called Jimmy Angel who spotted them from his plane in 1933.

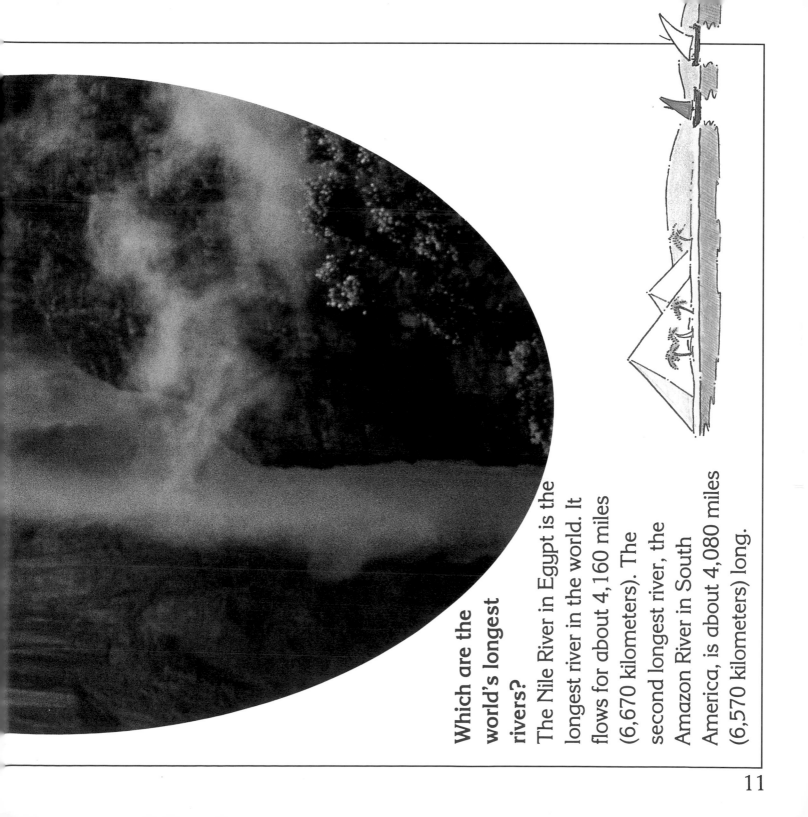

Which are the world's longest rivers?

The Nile River in Egypt is the longest river in the world. It flows for about 4,160 miles (6,670 kilometers). The second longest river, the Amazon River in South America, is about 4,080 miles (6,570 kilometers) long.

Which is the longest suspension bridge?

The Seto-Ohashi bridge links the islands of Honshu and Shikoku in Japan. It is the world's longest suspension bridge at over 7 miles (11 kilometers) in length. It was opened in 1988 and is built on two levels. There is a roadway for cars on top and a railroad underneath.

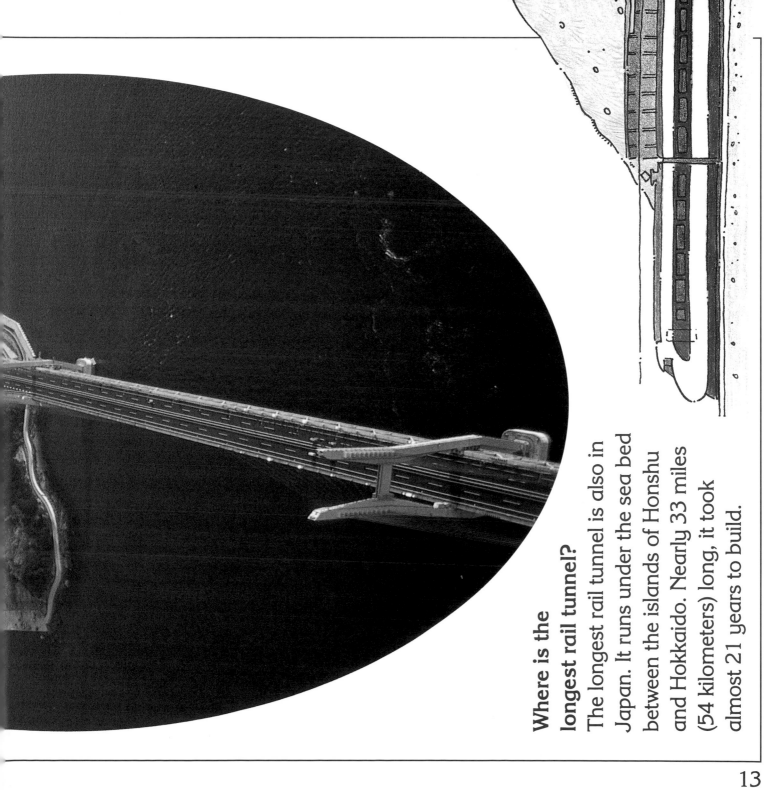

Where is the longest rail tunnel?

The longest rail tunnel is also in Japan. It runs under the sea bed between the islands of Honshu and Hokkaido. Nearly 33 miles (54 kilometers) long, it took almost 21 years to build.

13

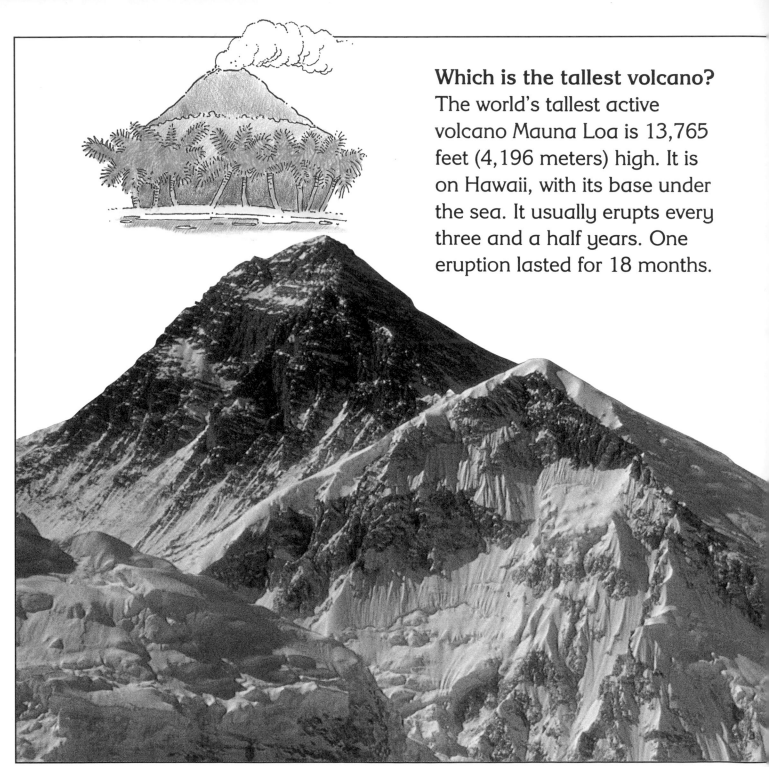

Which is the tallest volcano?
The world's tallest active volcano Mauna Loa is 13,765 feet (4,196 meters) high. It is on Hawaii, with its base under the sea. It usually erupts every three and a half years. One eruption lasted for 18 months.

Which is the tallest mountain?

Many people think Mount Everest in Asia is the tallest mountain. It isn't the tallest - but it is the highest above sea level, reaching 29,000 feet (8,848 meters) into the sky. Mauna Kea on the island of Hawaii has its base 20,000 feet (6,000 meters) under the sea. Over 13,000 feet (4,000 meters) of the mountain shows above the sea. This gives it a total height of 33,000 feet (10,203 meters), 4,000 feet (1,355 meters) taller than Mount Everest.

How tall is the tallest tree?

The tallest tree in the world is a redwood tree found in Redwood National Park in California. It measures an amazing 370 feet (113.7 meters) high. This is taller than 19 giraffes. Another huge redwood in the same park was blown over in a storm in 1991. It was just over 365 feet (111 meters) tall. Can you imagine the crash it made?

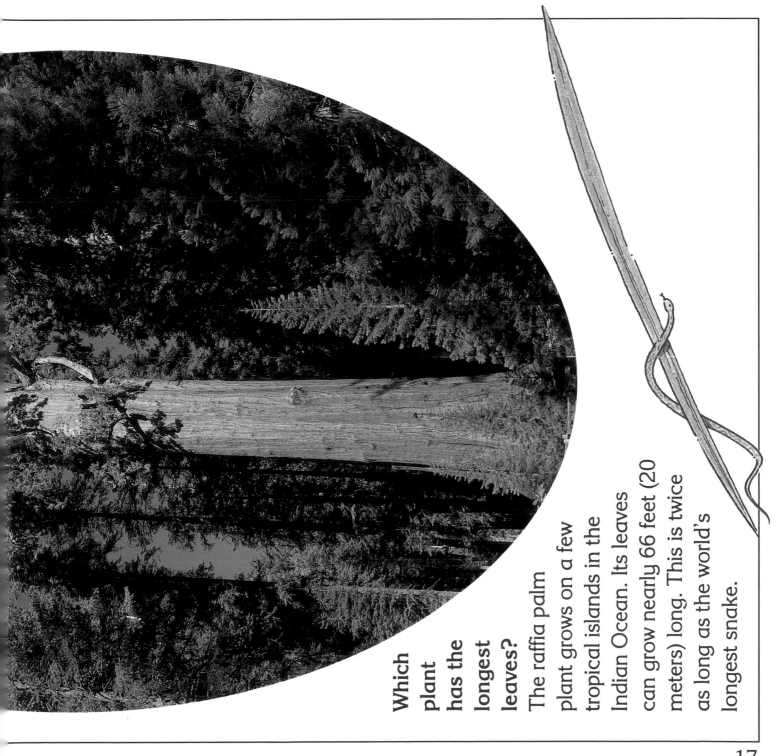

Which plant has the longest leaves?

The raffia palm plant grows on a few tropical islands in the Indian Ocean. Its leaves can grow nearly 66 feet (20 meters) long. This is twice as long as the world's longest snake.

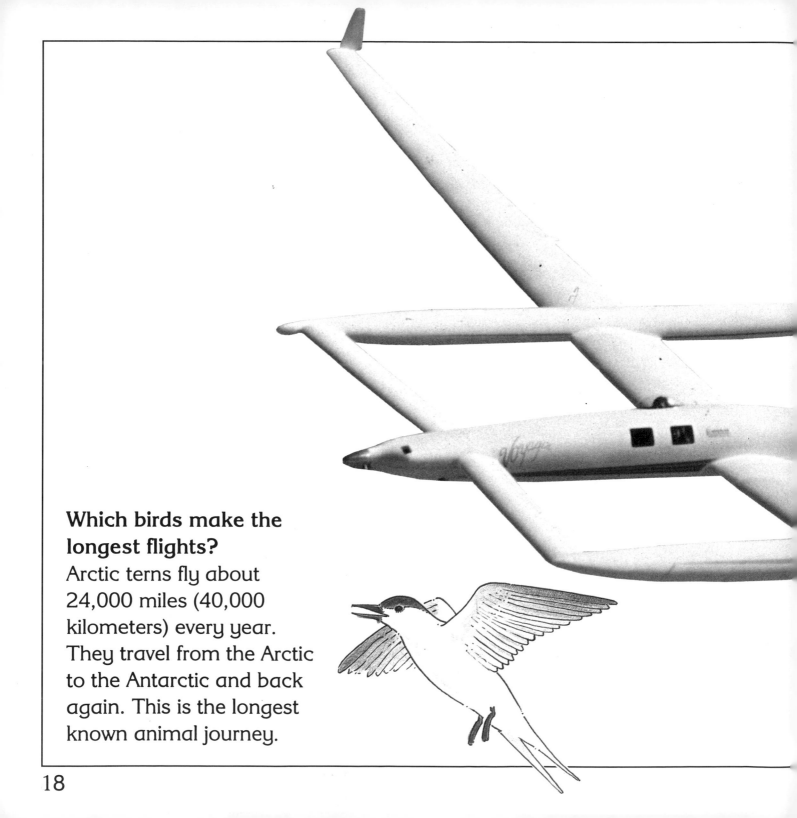

Which birds make the longest flights?

Arctic terns fly about 24,000 miles (40,000 kilometers) every year. They travel from the Arctic to the Antarctic and back again. This is the longest known animal journey.

Which was the longest plane flight?

In 1986 two American pilots became the first people to fly around the world without stopping for fuel. Their specially built plane was called Voyager. The flight took 9 days, 3 minutes and 44 seconds. They traveled a distance of 24,986 miles (40,212 kilometers).

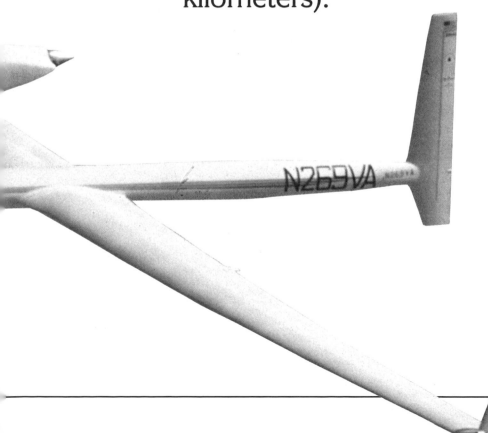

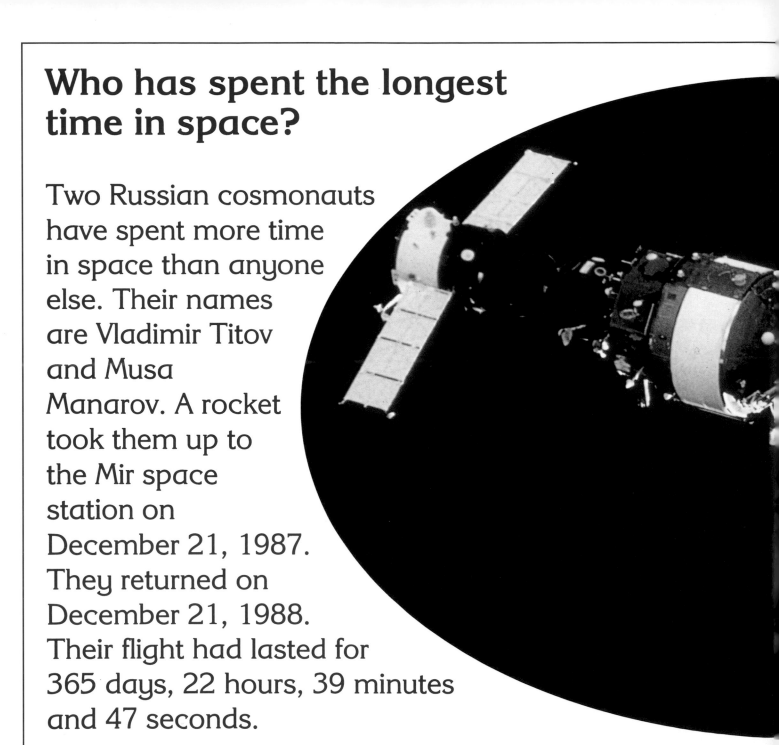

Who has spent the longest time in space?

Two Russian cosmonauts have spent more time in space than anyone else. Their names are Vladimir Titov and Musa Manarov. A rocket took them up to the Mir space station on December 21, 1987. They returned on December 21, 1988. Their flight had lasted for 365 days, 22 hours, 39 minutes and 47 seconds.

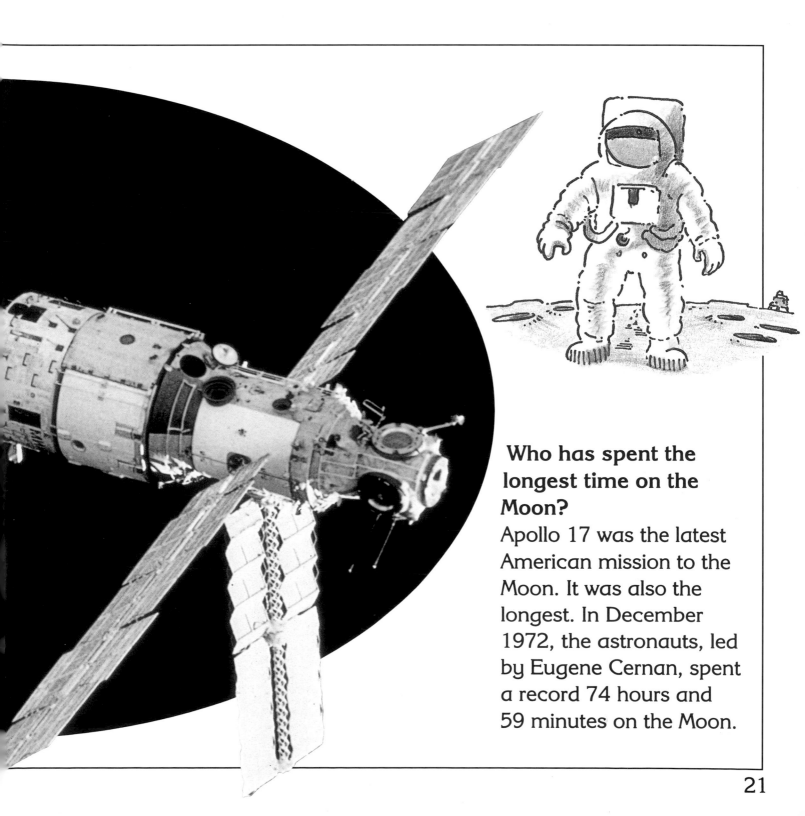

Who has spent the longest time on the Moon?

Apollo 17 was the latest American mission to the Moon. It was also the longest. In December 1972, the astronauts, led by Eugene Cernan, spent a record 74 hours and 59 minutes on the Moon.

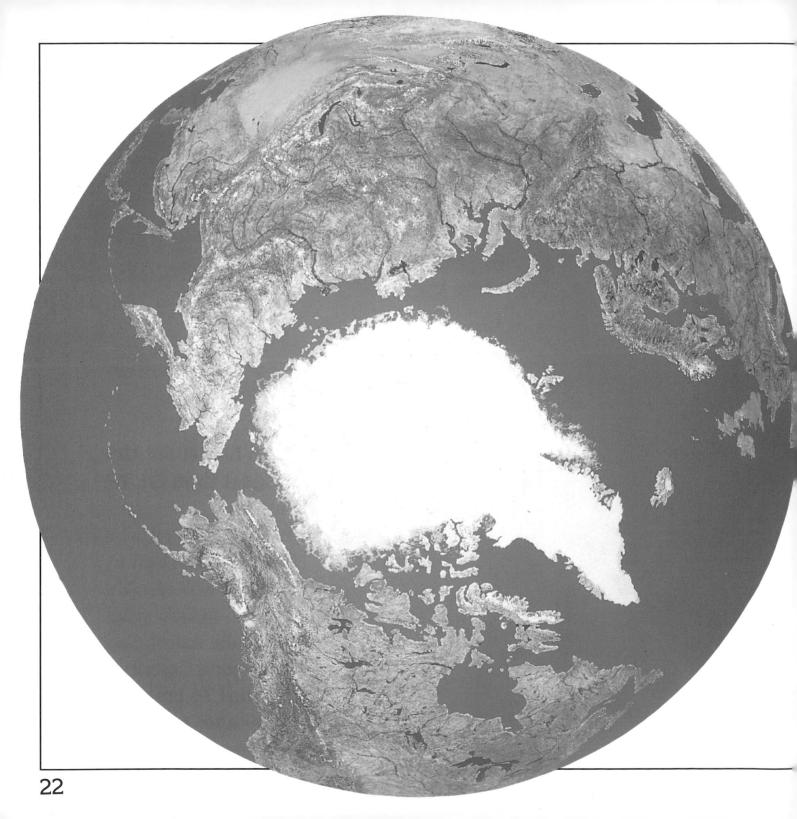

Which place has the longest day on Earth?

From June to July, the North Pole has daylight for 24 hours every day. The Sun shines all night, so it is called "the land of the midnight Sun." But from December to January, both day and night are dark and cold. From December to January, the South Pole has 24 hours of daylight at the other end of the world.

Which place has the longest day in the Solar System?
An Earth day lasts for 24 hours. This is how long it takes the Earth to spin around once on its axis. The planet Venus takes much longer to spin around. A day on Venus would last 243 Earth days.

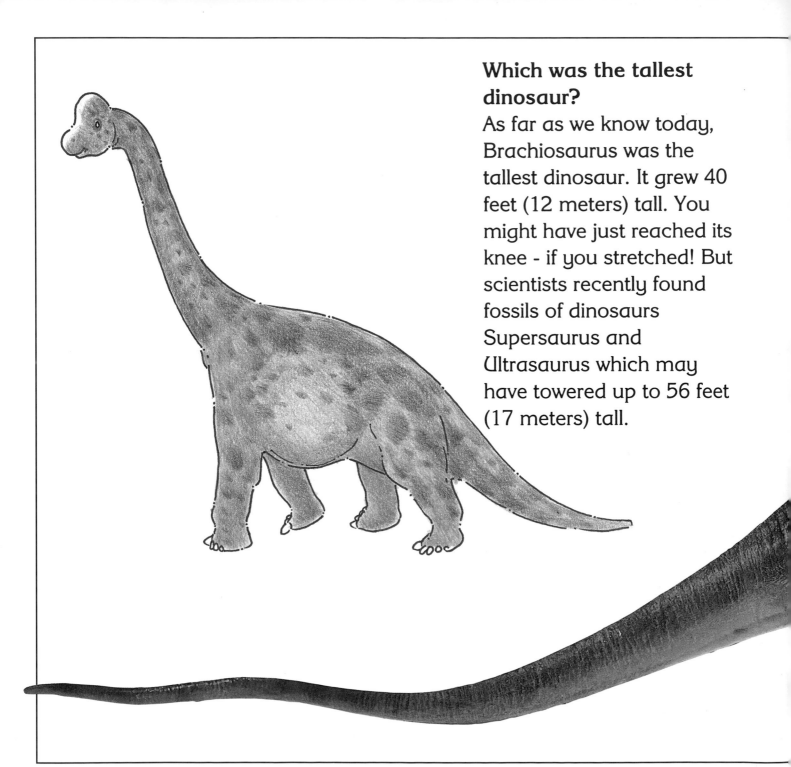

Which was the tallest dinosaur?

As far as we know today, Brachiosaurus was the tallest dinosaur. It grew 40 feet (12 meters) tall. You might have just reached its knee - if you stretched! But scientists recently found fossils of dinosaurs Supersaurus and Ultrasaurus which may have towered up to 56 feet (17 meters) tall.

Which was the longest dinosaur?

The longest dinosaur we know about was Diplodocus. It was as long as three buses. It had a long, snaky neck and a long, snaky tail. Even its footprints were long - about 3 feet (1 meter) from heel to toe. Despite its great length, Diplodocus probably weighed only about 9 tons as it had a very slim body.

How long is the longest car?

This crazy stretch limousine was built for movies and shows in Hollywood, California by Jay Ohrberg. Mr Ohrberg also owns the longest car ever made. It is 99 feet (30 meters) long and has 26 wheels. It also has a swimming pool and a small helicopter landing pad. It actually bends to go around corners.

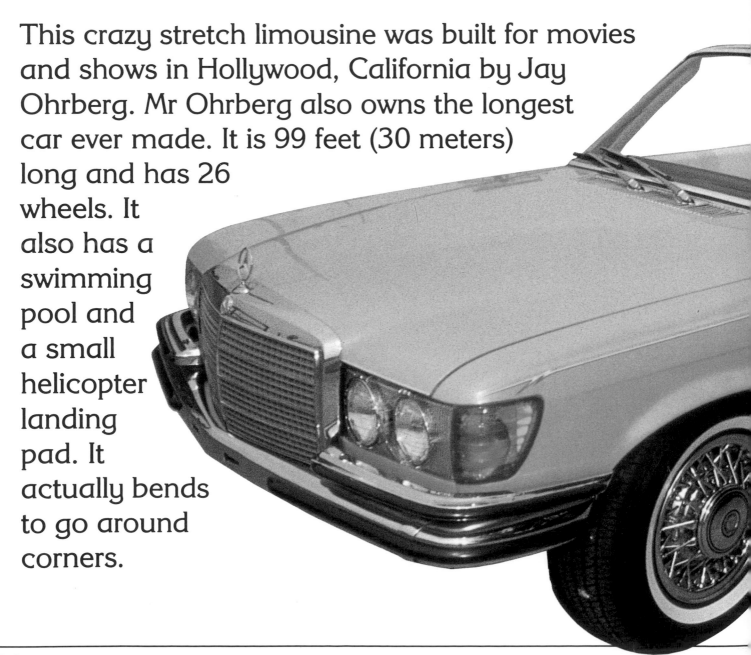

How many riders can sit on the longest bicycle?
Thirty five people can sit on the longest bicycle ever built. It is over 66 feet (20 meters) long and was built in Belgium.

Which is the longest musical instrument?

The alpenhorn must be one of the longest musical instruments. The longest alpenhorn ever was made in the United States in 1989. It is 155 feet (47 meters) long, nearly as long as an Olympic swimming pool. To play it, you have to blow into a mouthpiece. It must take a lot of breath! The sound takes about 0.1 seconds to travel through the horn and out the other end.

Which is the longest piece of music?

In 1952 a symphony called Victory at Sea was played in the USA. The performance lasted for about 13 hours. The longest non-stop piano piece lasts for over four hours. It is called "The Well-Tuned Piano" by La Monte Young.

Index

Photographs
Cover and pages 8-9, 10-11, 12-13, 18-19 and 26-27: Frank Spooner Pictures; title page and pages 16-17 and 28-29: Spectrum Colour Library; page 6: Planet Earth Pictures; pages 14-15, 20-21 and 22: Science Photo Library; page 24-25: Roger Vlitos.